"In *Still on the Cross*, Loretta Girzaitis and Richard L. Wood challenge themselves and all of us. But they do it in such a kind and encouraging way—with prose and verse—that the reader will not feel that it is the usual 'guilt trip.' At least this reader felt that the book was rather the beginning of a new awareness. In so many of the sick, oppressed, and suffering, Jesus is *still* on his cross."

John Powell, S.J.

"These meditations urge the reader to contemplate prayerfully the humanity of Jesus, his life and example. They call all to acknowledge and respond to the authentic cry of suffering in their immediate environment and to take up the cross daily to embrace God's will in the struggle for justice. They challenge everyone 'to be in the world' and to complete the task that Jesus has begun."

Sr. Thea Bowman, F.S.P.A.

"These poignant and faith-filled meditations invite us into the desperate passion of Jesus. Through the similar experiences of more recent followers, the poor and those trying to be poor, Loretta and Richard offer us rich spiritual companionship. Come along—not for the ride—but for the passion."

Richard Rohr, O.F.M.
Center for Action and Contemplation
Albuquerque, New Mexico

"It will be difficult not to pray as you read these beautifully written reflections for Lent. They embody the best of contemporary theology and spirituality. The call to conversion is urgent and the love of justice is deep. *'Tolle et lege!'*"

T. Howland Sanks, S.J.
Jesuit School of Theology at Berkeley

"Don't read—unless you can handle the challenge! In a time when the Gospel is too often equated with prosperity, success and beautiful people, it is good to read something which calls us back to essentials. I have never read anything more on target about what it means to be a Christian in our contemporary world."

Rev. Paul Lowder
United Methodist Minister
Greensboro, North Carolina

"...the authors craft, from their own faith and experience, a bridge that will take you from head to heart and from Jesus to your sisters and brothers."

Clarence Thomson
NCR Cassettes
Kansas City, Missouri

"These poems and reflections carve a path into the wilderness of Jesus' passion, death, and resurrection. We know the stories, the names of all the key players, the inexorable trajectory of events, but this book is an invitation to make the pilgrimage ourselves. The effect is neither to preach nor to explain, but to engage, as we try to discern where the path of our discipleship will lead us. The book deeply moved me."

Dr. Martha Stortz
Pacific Lutheran Theological Seminary

Loretta Girzaitis
Richard L. Wood

Meditations
on the
Human Condition
and the
Desperate Passion of Jesus

XXIII
TWENTY-THIRD PUBLICATIONS
Mystic, Connecticut

DEDICATION

We dedicate this book
to those who struggle for liberation—
political, economical, emotional, spiritual—
and who overcome their oppression
through action and love.

Second printing 1991

Twenty-Third Publications
185 Willow Street
P.O. Box 180
Mystic, CT 06355
(203) 536-2611
800-321-0411

ISBN 0-89622-449-x
Library of Congress Catalog Card Number 90-90306

Contents

Introduction

Lent invites us to reflect in a special way on a person's love that was so total and unconditional it led to his death. Lent is also a time when we need to examine our commitment to the Holy One's invitation to follow Jesus. How sincere are we in accepting this invitation? Do we pick what is pleasant and easy and ignore what demands sacrifice of us and even crucifixion? Are we as earnest about observing the Beatitudes as we are the Ten Commandments?

At some time or other, all of us experience doubt, insecurity, alienation, struggle, loneliness, and failure. We wonder if our lives have meaning. Have our efforts touched and influenced the lives of others? We wrestle with the responses to our dilemmas. We sense that wholeness eludes us when life becomes more fragmented than complete.

Because he was human, Jesus had experiences similar to ours. He suffered internal violence during his moments of crisis and uncertainty; he suffered external violence inflicted by those who could not control their fear and hate. When he stood upon his scaffold pinioned by iron pegs, he offered his pain to Abba, the Source of all being, who had sent him to a people lost in the mire of despair and indifference. His wrenching cries revealed the anguish he felt, and only Abba understood the depth of pain and submission voiced in his heart-rending prayers.

Yet his thoughts embraced those around him, even though his bolted arms could not. His final words became a permanent summons to compassion as well as an exclamation of the triumph of good.

We two authors share our reflections on the seven last statements of Jesus on the cross as recorded in the gospels. (The selections are from the *New American Bible* since this is the translation used in eucharistic liturgies.)

Each chapter maintains a pattern. There are three segments in each chapter, in addition to the biblical selection introducing it. The first is Jesus' expression of his wringing struggles to come to grips with the will of God. The next is a reflective essay focusing on possible contemporary implications of Jesus' expressive yearnings. Finally, a prayerful response to Jesus' anguish completes the chapter.

The reflections were written by Loretta Girzaitis and the essays by Richard L. Wood.

We focus primarily on Jesus' agony on the cross, but we also include reflections on Jesus' birth, which brings him into history, and on his baptism and proclamation at Nazareth, which plummet Jesus into his ministry. We end our reflections with the resurrection and ascension since these events close the chapter on Jesus' earthly life and challenge each Christian to complete the work Jesus has left undone.

We invite you to read each chapter slowly and prayerfully. Open yourself to whatever feelings surface. Feel free, in your imagination, to become Jesus and to feel as he felt. Let your insights guide you to a prayerful response.

But it is not enough simply to feel along with this loving friend. The power of Jesus' love was such that he spent his life seeking and carrying out God's will regardless of personal effort, uncertainty, and suffering. He boldly bids us to follow his example.

Can you accept his challenge to love as he has loved, to be one with him in bringing about the reign of the Holy One? This Lent, will you consciously determine the way you will live so that God's kingdom might be present in our midst?

Jesus' stance in the face of opposition models for us the difference between smallness and greatness. We make the decision either to seek God's will as we immerse ourselves into life, or to sink into the webs of our egos to be trapped there.

Lent is the time when we deliberately examine our lives to see how closely they are aligned to Christ's. Jesus has gone before us as the way; he claims we can walk the same road. It is up to us, as individuals and in community, to continue on the way he has journeyed.

May the images this book triggers become personal possibilities for you. Feel free to keep a journal as you respond to your loving Redeemer. If you are moved to share your reflections or prayers with either of the authors, you are invited to write to either or both of them via the publisher.

1

In those days Caesar Augustus published a decree ordering a census of the whole world. This first census took place while Quirinius was governor of Syria. Everyone went to register, each to his own town. And so Joseph went from the town of Nazareth in Galilee to Judea, to David's town of Bethlehem—because he was of the house and lineage of David—to register with Mary, his espoused wife, who was with child.

While they were there, the days of her confinement were completed. She gave birth to her first-born son and wrapped him in swaddling clothes and laid him in a manger, because there was no room for them in the place where travelers lodged. (Luke 2:1–7)

Born as an ordinary human being,
I entered earth
    encased in flesh,
    which has become my heritage
    forever.
    Within this strange environment,
    I grew in age,
    enjoying the challenge
    of continuous discovery.

I learned from
   the birds in the air
   and the lilies in the field.
Joseph's skill taught me a craft;
Miriam's love intensified my yearnings;
the village rabbi expanded my horizons.
   I stored up wisdom in my heart
   as I absorbed my inheritance
   from Abraham, Jacob, Moses, and David.

Living as a despised Nazarean,
I learned the hopelessness
   of the victimized and oppressed.
But through it all,
   I sought Abba's will,
   developed my talents,
   stepped into the place of others, tested myself.

Grace permeated my entire being,
   filled me with longing to liberate
   the sinful and the unjust,
     trapped in their pits
     of baubles and possessions.

It was Abba's insistent nudging
   that eventually
   called me forth to start the work
   I had been sent to do within humanity,
     in this limited space and time.

Will you accept partnership with me
   to eliminate the obstacles

that still hinder and prohibit
the existence of Abba's kingdom
on earth?

What a strange beginning to the life of Jesus Christ, Lord and Savior: the simplest of births in the shabbiest of places. Yet this birth hints at the very heart of the Christian message. Born in the most ordinary circumstances, Jesus is human, flesh and blood like all of us. But he is of the "house and lineage of David," as the Messiah had to be, according to Jewish tradition: a man and God.

Throughout the centuries, the church has captured this double reality of Jesus' identity in the formula "both fully human and fully divine." In faith, most of us have accepted the incarnation as expressing what we believe about Jesus. But what does it mean in our lives? Is it an empty concept, devoid of significance, that has been handed on by tradition? Or does it mean something vital and life-giving?

The meaning of the incarnation can provide us with the confidence in our relationship with God that we need for a living faith. But first we must get at the real tradition; we must make sure we understand it correctly and strip away the dead husks of false belief we have associated with Jesus for so long.

Too often we've known a kind of half-human and half-divine Jesus, sometimes a man, sometimes God—depending on who he chose to be—a kind of "revolving-door" Jesus. It is not the Christ of the tradition, nor the Jesus of Nazareth of the gospels. Jesus became, literally, fully human.

Or we've come to believe in Jesus as a "god-in-disguise," walking around in a human body, dressed in human clothing, pretending to face all the trials of humanity, a "superman Jesus." But Jesus was a human being. As unadorned and severe as that sounds, this man Jesus is the dominant image in the gospels, the one defended by the Christian tradition for centuries.

If we wish to believe in the Jesus who walked our world, we need to chew on this reality, digest it, and take it in as our own: Jesus was born of woman, just like each of us; he truly became flesh. As such, he faced all the trials, aches, and yearnings each of us faces.

Yet, this is only half the story. The church confesses always that Jesus is also the Christ, the Messiah. Somehow, in ways we only begin to understand, this human Jesus was truly God. Somehow he lived in such intimate union with God that he could only be explained as God-among-us: Emmanuel.

Only the incorporation of both sides of Jesus' identity gives us the confidence to live in faith. His full humanity allows us to identify with him in all our joys and pains, yearnings, hopes, and fears. It allows us to believe that he shared our burdens and embraced our brokenness. A God who was only god could do none of that, and so could not offer any ultimate hope for us in our human condition. Such a god could only invite us to escape our humanness. This Jesus invites us to take on our humanness as fully as he did.

Jesus' full divinity allows us to trust that, in identifying with him, we have access to the fullness of life only God can provide. In knowing God so profoundly—that he *is* God—Jesus becomes a channel to that same experience of intimacy with the Father and Mother of all life.

A Jesus who was only human could do none of that, and so could offer us no hope to transcend our brokenness and egoism. But this Jesus-God invites us not only to accept our limitedness but also to transcend it as we encounter God and reach out to others. He offers hope and testimony that this is indeed possible.

An invitation to hope...hope in our daily lives and in the ultimate meaningfulness of our struggles and our world. In this very simple story of a common birth in Bethlehem, we are offered the beginnings of this most extraordinary invitation.

Me?
    fragile of will,
    fearful of failure,
    full of desire for power, success, fame?
How can I follow your way
    when I am fraught with
    weakness, failure, and insignificance?

You ask me to be liberator with you.
Can't you see that it is I
    who am the sinner?
Do you want me to taint
    the kingdom of Abba
    with my leaning
    toward selfishness, injustice, oppression?

I opt for the pleasures I deserve.
To reject, relinquish, surrender
    what I've earned through sweat and tears
        is foolishness.
I need satisfaction and security.

It comforts me.

Yes,
  I acknowledge your overtures:
    "Go sell what you have,
      give to the poor";
    "Take up your cross,
      follow me";
    "Love one another
      as I have loved you."
How can I accede to these requests
  when they are so demanding?

Yet, your birth within our realm
  shatters my complacency.
  You never let me go.

Like a hunter on my trail,
  you pursue me with your grace,
  inviting me to join the ranks with you
    to seek justice,
    practice solidarity,
    serve the poor.

Why do I run from you?
  I slow my pace.
Dear hunter, capture me,
  ignite within me the fire of your love.
Lead me to the greatness found in your infinity.

I submit.
  I will do what you ask of me.

2

When all the people were baptized and Jesus was at prayer after likewise being baptized, the skies opened and the Holy Spirit descended on him in visible form like a dove. A voice from heaven was heard to say: "You are my beloved Son. On you my favor rests."

Jesus, full of the Holy Spirit, then returned from the Jordan and was conducted by the Spirit into the desert for forty days, where he was tempted by the devil. During that time he ate nothing and at the end of it he was hungry. The devil said to him, "If you are the Son of God, command this stone to turn into bread." Jesus answered him, "Scripture has it,

'Not on bread alone shall man live.'"

Then the devil took him higher and showed him all the kingdoms of the world in a single instant. He said to him, "I will give you all this power and the glory of these kingdoms; the power has been given to me and I give it to whomever I wish. Prostrate yourself in homage before me, and it shall all be yours. In reply, Jesus said to him, "Scripture has it,

'You shall do homage to the Lord your God;
him alone shall you adore.'"

Then the devil led him to Jerusalem, set him on the parapet of the temple, and said to him, "If you are the Son of God, throw

yourself down from here, for Scripture has it,
  'He will bid his angels watch over you';
  and again,
  'With their hands they will support you,
    that you may never stumble on a stone.' "
Jesus said to him in reply, "It also says, 'You shall not put the Lord your God to the test.' "
When the devil had finished all the tempting he left him, to await another opportunity. (Luke 3:21–22; 4:1–13)

My time of waiting was finished.
A rumor abounded everywhere:
  a wild man was baptizing
    along the River Jordan,
    calling everyone to repentance.

There was an urgency within me
  to join those hordes,
  to become one of them,
  to submit myself
  to the cleansing of that water.

I sought to find the baptizer.
  John's booming energy
    drew me as a magnet.
  The waters engulfed me.

I attested my oneness
  with Abba's created family.
Abba danced
  and shouted with joy:
    "This is my beloved Son."

I had sealed my destiny.
After Abba's affirmation,
    there was no turning back.

Instead, Abba's Spirit led me into the desert,
    that fallow wilderness
    devoid of any nurture.
There my will was
    tempered, strengthened,
    as the evil one unleashed the weapons
    he sensed would destroy my integrity.

He insisted
    I turn stone into bread.
How senseless!
How stupid!
    Whom would this help but me?
    My hunger was manageable,
        but there were those whose bellies screamed for food.
    How would stone-turned-into-bread feed them?
Humanity needed to be primed and fed
    with the Word from Abba.
If this Word were chewed for nourishment,
    then all would love enough
    and there would be
    sufficient food for all to eat.

Once more he tried.
How idiotic!
    Ages ago,
        the evil one had worshipped Abba.
    Having lost that privilege,

he now promises me power
if I worship him.
This is laughable indeed!
Why should my authority
be offered as a gift
to one who has no claim on me?
The strength that lies within will shatter
hatred, control, and domination,
for the mighty will be deposed from their thrones
and
the lowly will be raised to take their places.
To give up my power to assume his
would allow him to dominate at will.
That temptation is a mockery,
unworthy of my attention.

How inept this tempter is!
Still unsure of my identity
and
giddy with his importance,
he offers another folly:
"If you are the Son of God,
throw yourself from the temple's pinnacle.
Angels will protect you."

And what will that prove, evil one?
That you can bring me to this height,
only to let me fall within your shadow?
I have not come to earth
to be a commanding, triumphant leader;
my glory lies in suffering and death.

Begone, my wicked enemy.
　I defy you,
　　and reject your patronage and despotism.
I refuse to be diminished by your tyranny.
I return to Nazareth, sustained by Abba's power.

Beloved... tempted....These words are central to Luke's story of the start of Jesus' public life and they lie at the heart of the experience of following Jesus today.

Before all else, the Christian life is a call to accept our belovedness before God. Jesus invites us to share in the intimate love of the one he called Father, or more accurately translated, "Papa" (Abba). It is a love so intimate that Luke can express it only in the language of parenthood: "You are my beloved Son."

We stand before God in the same kind of belovedness. We are loved beyond all reason and before anything we do to "earn" that love. Following Jesus means accepting the reality of this boundless love. In the security of this love we come to know forgiveness for our failure to love. Knowing that we stand beloved, we are freed from the fears that restrain us and we gain the power to be agents of love to the people and the world around us.

Freedom and the power to be agents of love... gifts.... But they come accompanied by many temptations to abuse them. As a human being, Jesus was tempted all his life in the same way we are. It is in his confrontation with some of these temptations that Luke depicts Jesus during his trial in the desert.

After forty days of fasting, Jesus is famished and, therefore, tantalized to "turn stones into bread." This first temptation is one of selfishness: to place personal needs before all else. It is not that our needs are unimportant, but sometimes they simply do not have top priority.

In Matthew's account, after the devil leaves Jesus, "angels came and ministered to him," taking care of his needs. This is, of course, what happens to us. When we put our needs first, we soon find them to be a bottomless pit and in our selfishness we create new "needs." But when we place God's will and the building of God's reign first, we allow our needs to be met within that commitment.

The second temptation deals with power. It is ironic: in accepting God's priorities we are given new power as agents of love; yet, this power is precisely one of the great temptations. The power we are called to exercise in building God's reign is power *with* others, the power of mutual collaboration and respect for each person's integrity. This power is never coercive; it always accepts the freedom of the other. It nurtures new life and allows the first fruits of that life to sprout and grow in the fresh air of freedom.

The power inherent in Jesus' temptation—and ours—is the power born of giving in to the lures of evil. It is the power of compulsion and coercion, the tools of the enemy of freedom. This is power *over* others, and its use always violates the integrity of the other.

The third temptation, toward a cavalier and irresponsible emancipation, perverts our freedom. On the Temple parapet Jesus was tempted to emancipate himself, to become totally independent. He recognized that this kind of "freedom" leads to meaningless efforts to manipulate rather than serve others.

In the temptation to be self-sufficient we, too, need to acknowledge that this leads to self-seeking and away from loving others. Focused on itself, this selfish liberation is disconnected from the concrete struggles of those who need our compassion.

Responsible freedom, on the other hand, responds graciously to God's generosity and strives to see itself multiplied in the freedom of others. True freedom struggles to beget additional freedoms. Grounded in God, it transcends itself by reaching out to others.

Temptations to selfishness, power, and irresponsibility lurk everywhere, even in our best-intentioned efforts to serve. They can overwhelm us unless we confront them the way Jesus did: within the context of accepting God's complete love. We are beloved, even when we are tempted. In our belovedness, we can find the strength to be true to our call.

Dear Lord Jesus,
    we, too, have been baptized,
    saturated with the grace of Abba,
      and so,
as your sisters and brothers,
    we have been accepted
    as members of your family,
    carrying the royal name of Christian.

Abba may not publicly affirm us,
    but the call is there
        to step outside our selfishness,
        to recognize the dignity within self and others,
        to acknowledge that this invitation is divine:
        to love our neighbors without limit.

Because cleansing strengthened you,
    drove you into the wilderness to discern Abba's will,
    we appreciate your election to be
        our mentor,
        our examplar,
        our friend.

Likewise must we go into our deserts
    to face enticement,
    to meet allurement,
    to deal with the evil that seduces.

Temptation is a mania
    demanding custody of our deepest selves.
Disguised as merit,
    it creates desires
    that consume virtue, nobility, and holiness,
    bequeathing contamination and corruption.

It attempts to tip the balance
      between
    light and darkness,
    healing and suffering,
    heaven and earth.

It is only
    when its ashes form the silt
      from which goodness rises
    that we regain the constancy we need
    to cling to you, Beloved One,
    so as to
      walk your way,

seek your truth,
covet your love.

How foolish it would be
to walk our wayward ways,
ignoring the strength
that you bestow
upon those who choose
to journey on the way
with you.

Be with us, Holy One,
as we join your campaign
to be and to do
what you require.

3

[Jesus] came to Nazareth where he had been reared, and entering the synagogue on the sabbath as he was in the habit of doing, he stood up to do the reading. When the book of the prophet Isaiah was handed him, he unrolled the scroll and found the passage where it was written:

"The Spirit of the Lord is upon me;
    therefore, he has anointed me.
He has sent me to bring glad tidings to the poor,
    to proclaim liberty to captives,
Recovery of sight to the blind,
    and release to prisoners,
To announce a year of favor from the Lord."

Rolling up the scroll he gave it back to the assistant and sat down. All in the synagogue had their eyes fixed on him. Then he began by saying to them, "Today this Scripture passage is fulfilled in your hearing." All who were present spoke favorably of him; they marveled at the appealing discourse which came from his lips. (Luke 4:16–22)

The Spirit of the Lord
    is upon me

and
   I am its bearer.
I was conceived by the Spirit
   in the womb of Mary,
anointed and confirmed by her
   in the River Jordan.
The Spirit empowers me.

I stand before you,
   my beloved friends,
      in this place
         and
      at this moment
as I stood before my kinfolk
   in the synagogue in Nazareth.

The time of then and now is the same,
   for the message needs continuous repeating:
Give to the poor
   of your abundance,
      so that
   in this equality and justice,
   poverty will be eradicated.

Release captives;
   loose the fetters of their restraints
      so that,
   through your mercy,
   they might be given another chance.

Heal the oppressed,
   broken in body and spirit
      so that,

through your healing,
   they, too, might have life.
Forgive your debtors,
   abolish their debts,
   forget the hurts they have inflicted
      so that
   they might start anew.

Exploitation must stop!

This is the edict:
   I have come to preach the Good News
      not as a dream for the future
      but as a new era that begins right now.

There is no hidden agenda here. At the onset of his ministry, Jesus proclaims it in crystal-clear terms: "glad tidings to the poor...liberty to captives...to announce a year of favor from the Lord." As co-workers in this mission, we are invited to share our gifts and the freedom of God's love.

This invitation is not to exclusive love, as if the rich or the middle class are beyond God's affection. But we are asked to love preferentially, to place first those who most need our help, those whom Jesus placed first: the poor, the prisoners, those who are captive in a world created for freedom.

We can choose to decline this invitation. God does not compel us; we are always free to accept or not. But the invitation beckons relentlessly, like the images of the poor that filter into our lives as we watch the news or walk downtown. "Follow me," Jesus says. "Allow your life to open the eyes of those who will not see; bring good news to the poor. Follow me."

Yes, we can choose not to follow this calling, but such evasion can only end in isolation and loneliness, for it is an escape from others and from God in order to retreat into ourselves. Down this path lies death. But Jesus invites us to life, filling up and spilling over into the lives of others.

Can we accept this invitation, even if it leads to crucifixion, the path that Jesus took? If we follow it, it will lead to a fuller life for us and for others.

My Lord,
    what an inaugural address!

Finally,
    your time has come
    to lay out your plans
    for your work of salvation.

This message of yours, this
    stark,
    shocking,
    powerful
request for reversal
demands social change,
    a liberation from bondage,
    a restructuring of relationships.
It shakes up the status quo
    and leads resistance and rebellion.

Yet it gives hope
    to the battered and discarded,
    for you announce
    God's sovereign reign for all:

the rich and the poor,
the oppressor and the oppressed,
the foolish and the wise
now,
today.

Lord, if we are to take you
at your word,
then,
we have to let go of many of our possessions
to distribute them equally with those who lack
the basic necessities of life,
so that there will no longer be any poor.

You ask us to be
compassionate and understanding to prisoners,
many of whom are jailed
because they courageously speak out against
oppression, aggression, and injustice.
You request us to seek their release,
regardless of the consequences to ourselves.

You encourage us to lift up
the crushed, humiliated, and rejected,
and
to provide them with the means
of respect, dignity, and honor
they deserve.

You make it clear, Lord,
that we need to choose
between God and Mammon
if we are to hear the Good News you offer us.

The choice to be part of your company
   means we either join the ranks of the
   poor, blind, captive, and oppressed
      or
   work radically to change their conditions
      by removing injustices and inequalities,
      by lifting up the unfortunate and marginalized,
      by providing sight to those who can't see,
      by freeing all from bondage.

Your request
   to make everything equal for everybody,
   rattles, frightens, and alarms
   our very depths.
We shake as anxiety terrifies our senses.
How can we relinquish the tinsel that is ours?

And if we risk
   allotting possessions to others with love,
   confronting oppressors with courage,
   delivering the imprisoned with compassion,
   forgiving debts with mercy,
      then
   will the Good News
      seep into the substance of our spirits?
      weave itself into the fabric of our hearts?
      dwell within the hollow of our minds?

If that is the gift you bestow,
   we will do our best.
We promise you,
   we will struggle to proclaim the acceptable year,
   so that the Spirit of the Lord would be upon us, too.

4

Jesus was led away, and carrying the cross by himself, went out to what is called the Place of the Skull (in Hebrew, Golgotha). There they crucified him, and two others with him, one on either side, Jesus in the middle. Pilate had an inscription placed on the cross which read,

Jesus, the Nazorean,
the king of the Jews. (John 19:16–19)

Wood was my friend in the carpenter shop
    when Joseph taught me this creative trade.
Yet, today as wood is laid
    upon my broken and lacerated back,
        it is my enemy.
Its weight bears down upon the wounds
    and sucks the blood from out my veins.
It leaves me helpless and collapsed.

To become human,
    to bear the challenge of this fragile life,
    is my destiny.
Within, my body, mind, and spirit are coalescing
    all the yearnings, dreams, evil, and pain

of all of humankind
   and so,
tethered like a colt,
deprived of freedom,
   subject to ridicule and intimidation,
I surrender to the slaughter
   as a first-born lamb.
The words of Abba,
   "You are my beloved,"
   preserve my spirit.
The sin of the world envelops me,
   but love, more than nails,
   clamps me to this tree.

As demons taunt, temptation surfaces
   to rid myself of pain, demand relief.
Yet, memories of childhood lessons
   learned about the wood, alive with sap,
   give sustenance to hope.
The strength within the tree
   is found in me.
This dead wood extinguishes my human existence,
   yet sets me free for life again.

The cross on which Jesus was nailed—does it have any real meaning in our lives today, or has it simply become another empty image? We declare in our creed that Jesus Christ died for our sins, that we are forgiven, but do we feel within us the freedom of that claim?

Often we avoid facing the crucifixion of Jesus or we simply take it for granted; we frequently refuse to make it a living part of our faith. When we take it for granted, we see it as an event of the past, where it becomes a distant echo, devoid of real power to transform our lives. Then Jesus is made impotent and only whispers to us across the centuries. What can we do to allow him to call us boldly here and now, at our moment in history?

To hear the cry of freedom in all its power, we must permit Jesus' crucifixion to come alive for us again. If we allow his crucifixion to be united with all the real suffering, in flesh and spirit, that we encounter in our lives and our world, both the crucifixion and our suffering will be transformed. The crucifixion will cease to be an empty symbol of the past, and our present pain will call us to tear down the other crosses we have built into our lives.

The crosses of our lives...they are all around us and we feel their nails in our flesh, yet we continue building them. Whenever we feel inadequate in our work, our family life, and our struggles to love, we allow these failings to overwhelm us. Then, unable truly "to choose life," we lead lives that edge along toward meaninglessness.

And then there are the crosses in the rest of the world: the wars, the starvation, the racism and repression. These are meaningless deaths on a scale we can scarcely imagine and so we feel powerless to deal with them.

Meaningless lives in the suburbs, in the churches, in our homes. Meaningless deaths in El Salvador, Israel, Lebanon, Northern Ireland, and in the urban jungles of the United States and Canada. These slabs of personal and global meaninglessness today form the cross on which the world hangs in agony, joined to the suffering of Jesus.

Can we honestly envision this cross, the true cross of our time? Do we allow Jesus to give us the courage and the faith to dream the dreams that will lead us beyond this cross toward the ongoing resurrection of our lives and the world?

We yearn to hear Jesus' call, but we will hear it fully only if we allow his crucifixion to come alive within us once more, in all its threatening power. This is not the theology of glorifying suffering and sacrifice again and again. Rather, it is a remembrance of Jesus' death drawing together all the pain throughout the ages, our own included.

This is Jesus' invitation to us: to face our pain and fears and to allow ourselves to be transformed and made new once again, for freedom and for service.

Jesus, I am decoyed daily
    by the allurements of this world,
    fearful of the dedication that love invokes.
I frequently refuse
    to bear my cross along with you.
I resist suffering
    those holes in hands, and feet, and heart.

The crossbeams are ugly and demeaning;
    their splinters dig and burn with gnawing pain
        within the essence of my being
        when my heart is drained and empty of your grace.

But when you are bolted to this dead wood,
    your hope is mine,
        for your blood promises entitlement
        to friendship, love, and pardon.
That hope, even in my resistance,
    allures me
    and draws me near.

Your cross enfolds both time and space,
    linking me to the Holy One
        and to all who
        inhabit this earth.
Even if I am afraid,
    how can I refuse
    to bear this cross of daily living
    when it assures me of union,
    a union beyond my wildest expectations?
I set aside my apprehension
        and
    wed myself to you today,
even if I be crucified with you.

5

Near the cross of Jesus there stood his mother, his mother's sister, Mary, the wife of Clopas, and Mary Magdalene. Seeing his mother there with the disciple whom he loved, Jesus said to his mother, "Woman, there is your son." In turn, he said to the disciple, "There is your mother." From that hour onward, the disciple took her into his care. (John 19:25–27)

Behold your son; behold your mother.

Woman,
    as you stand atop this ridge,
    enveloped in your net of pain,
    where do your memories take you?

Are you reliving
    those awesome moments
    when you agreed to bring me into being?

Are you searching
    the town of David
    to find some privacy for birth?

Are you adjusting
   to life as a refugee
   in the land that enslaved our ancestors?

Are you quivering
   with fright
   as you search for a delinquent adolescent?

Are you chuckling
   at your strategy in Cana
   that galvanized me into action?

Are you renewing
   your courage
   to let me go about Abba's business?

The time for farewells has come,
   beloved woman.
   The fruit of your womb is being harvested.

The flesh that you
   so frequently carressed
   is mangled on this wood.

The blood that you alone
   bequeath to me
   is hallowing this ground.

Woman,
   there can be no other way.
   Life with you is culminated.

In this crazed and flaming moment,
    I will you to humanity.

My dear friend John,
    as you stand alongside this woman of courage,
    immersed within your thoughts,
        where do your memories take you?

Are you recalling
    your doubts and your fear
    as you responded to the invitation to follow me?

Are you remembering
    the competition between you and the others
    that sometimes caused dissension
    and misunderstanding?

Are you regenerating
    the ecstasy on that mountain set apart
    when Moses and Elijah joined us in glory?

Are you accepting
    the terms of love
    proposed at our final dinner last night?

Are you cringing with shame and remorse
    at the thought of your weakness
    in the garden?

Why do you stand beneath this tree,
    when all of my friends
    have abandoned me?

The time to say farewell has come.
My work is done;
   I must move on.

This woman stands in anguish rent,
   the final sword has pierced her soul.
Find space within your heart, dear friend,
   to love my mother as your own.

———————

Throughout his ministry, Jesus' companions were drawn together because of his presence and power. Only later would they understand that this power was really God's presence in him. They joined Jesus' band not because they were initially drawn to one another but because they were drawn to Jesus. His presence made them a community and gave them their identity.

Now, suddenly, Jesus was on a cross, taken away from them. He who had drawn them together was apparently abandoning them. In their confusion and uncertainty, they deserted him. They had left everything to build their world around him. Now everything seemed lost. Those who have lost a loved one through separation or death know the utter desolation and agony of such a loss.

The only two who set aside their fear, doubt, and pain and joined Jesus beneath the cross were Mary, the mother of Jesus, and John, the beloved disciple. "Behold your son." "Behold your mother." Jesus calls them from desperation into a new relatedness, a direct love each for the other. Their love can no longer pass only through Jesus, indirectly drawing them closer to each other. They must love fully, directly, accepting each other as kin in the most concrete, real sense. "You *are* son; you *are* mother."

So we today must move beyond our theories of "loving all people because they are our brothers and sisters" or because "they are the images of Christ." We have allowed these abstractions to stand in the way of a real flesh-and-blood encounter with God in our midst. These theories are motives *why* we are called to love one another; they are not the love itself.

The love we are called to is a direct love, an affirmation and acceptance of the other as kin, just as John and Mary were called to it. Like them, we are summoned to this committed love precisely at the place in our lives and our world where there is suffering. For Mary and John this was in the utter devastation they felt at the crucifixion of their beloved Jesus.

We, too, encounter suffering in our lives, where precisely we must love. As we experience disintegrating families living in ruptured relationships, disoriented youth searching for meaning, materialistic midlifers absorbed in the ordinary, or the aged lonely in their abandonment, we must love.

We must love even those we cannot see: the oppressed and persecuted of El Salvador, the Philippines, China, and on the streets and reservations of our own country. They are present in our world, urgently present. In loving them, we will learn to see them. Jesus' challenge is to love them directly, here and now, as equals.

We do not pity the suffering, for pity implies superiority. We love them because we believe in God's redeeming presence, even at the brink of the abyss. That presence was with Jesus on the cross; it is in those suffering in our world today.

In our spiritual blindness we may refuse to recognize

God in the weak and the poor. And so we may turn away from directly loving one another.

Every time we mouth well-meaning but hazy expressions of concern for the hungry people of Downtown, U.S.A., Central America, Africa, or other impoverished areas of the world without taking action, we drug ourselves. We refuse to love. It is as if we feel we can rush headlong into Easter without passing through the suffering of Good Friday.

Do we believe in this man-God who calls us from his cross to kinship, to direct love?

Do we believe that in his willingness to embrace his personal cross Jesus was freed for the fullness of the resurrection?

Do we believe that in turning to others in their suffering because we trust that Jesus is present in them we, too, are freed for that fullness of life?

O Holy One, today we stand where Mary and John stood, at the feet of the crucified ones of our day. Call us beyond ourselves to love here and now.

———————————

Mary, John, Jesus,
    human trinity,
        your raw valor in these last moments together
        saturates us with your love,
        elevates us to where we are called to be.

As we stand with you upon this ridge,
    spur us to embrace the world you love so much.

Challenge our neglect of others
    when we disregard their needs.

Support us as we learn by heart
    the lessons of compassion.

Then send us forth
    as envoys,
    as couriers of your love.

6

*Two others who were criminals were led along with him to be cru-
cified. When they came to Skull Place, as it was called, they crucified him there and the criminals as well, one on his right and the
other on his left. [Jesus said, "Father forgive them; they do not
know what they are doing."] (Luke 23:32–34)*

Forgive them...

As the ages pass in review before us, Abba,
   I hang here before you,
   saturated by pain.
I am pinioned by the
   lies, rapes, jealousies,
   murder, hatred, and revenge
     that lacerate the human race
       and continue with unbroken rhythm.

Their staccato beat is harsh,
   unfurling defiance,
   embracing hatred,
   denying reprieve.
What is there
   that you and I have not witnessed?

Can anyone surprise us
   with new wickedness?

Forgiveness is in order,
   Abba, Source of all Love,
   or my blood bath will be in vain.
Stupidity, ignorance, and selfishness
   lure these fragile beings
   into voids that envelop them.
   They really don't know what they're doing!

Jesus' cry on the cross was the cry of the innocent one: "Father, forgive them; they do not know what they are doing." Those in authority, who were threatened by Jesus' witness to the truth and to the good in the world, killed him.

Jesus was so intimately in touch with the sin in people's lives that he could name and denounce its presence. When people had faith, he healed them of their sins. He also freed them from the law, for it had become an instrument of oppression rather than of freedom. In the end, those in authority executed Jesus because he challenged their abuses.

Father, forgive them, for they knew not what they did.

Jesus walks in North America today, as he promised he would. He is present in all people, regardless of their social or economic status. Because his presence is harder to discern in some people, we must learn to see him in the downtrodden, the unemployable, the physically impaired, the mentally disadvantaged, the homeless, alcoholics, foreclosed farmers, AIDS victims, the elderly infirm—these are Jesus in our lives. We may fail even to see them at all, much less see Christ in them.

Forgive us, O God, we know not what we do.

Jesus walks in our world today, as he promised he would. He is alive in those Third World people who are disinherited of their land, their livelihood, and their dignity by the economic decisions of powerful consumer nations, such as ours. He thirsts with the landless Brazilian peasant, hungers with the Mexican factory worker paid three dollars a day, suffers with black South Africans, screams in rage in El Salvador. Jesus is present in the anguish of the Indian people of Guatemala who see death squads assassinate their leaders, and whose children are forced to seek refuge in foreign lands.

Forgive us, O God, we know not what we do.

Our daily news brings us word of the violence committed in the land where Jesus lived. The Lord is really there today with the Palestinians engulfed in grief over family members killed in the streets. Their deaths test our own moral fiber, because our tax dollars are spent on the bullets that kill them.

Forgive us, gracious God, for though we begin to see
  what we are doing,
  we continue doing it.

O suffering Jesus,
  your tender compassion draws me to surrender to you
  and to rage at injustice's dark night.

I neither understand nor feel at ease
  with your total, unlimited love
  which pursues my hardened and divided heart
  to strip it of its pride.

I am blinded by contemporary allurements,
    bribed by power and prestige.
Possessions unravel the fabric of my spirit
    to hasten its collapse.
Liberate me from the bondage that is mine.

Forgive me,
    acquit me,
        grant me amnesty.

7

*One of the criminals hanging in crucifixion blasphemed him:
"Aren't you the Messiah? Then save yourself and us." But the
other one rebuked him: "Have you no fear of God, seeing you are
under the same sentence? We deserve it, after all. We are only
paying the price for what we have done, but this man has done
nothing wrong." He then said, "Jesus, remember me when you
enter upon your reign." And Jesus replied, "I assure you: this day
you will be with me in paradise." (Luke 23:39–43)*

This day you will be with me in paradise...

Three men hang on the rim of a hill,
    portraits etched in air,
    targets for the venom from below.
Soon that target narrows,
    as shafts of ridicule and hatred
    converge upon the center:
        "Save yourself and us!"

A sneer from the left breaks through:
    "The three of us are lawbreakers,
    seeking freedom from oppression.

They call you the 'Messiah';
then why are you suspended here?
  Get yourself down;
  pick up the sword;
  destroy the Roman dog."

This verbal blow is overshadowed
  by the innocence
  of the man on the right.
    "Why couldn't I have met him earlier?
    As I tremble on this platform of death,
    what else is left to me but hope?
    Perhaps there's meaning even here!"

Seeing the man's faith, Jesus promises him paradise "this very day." Right now. This promise is not only for this one man dying alongside Jesus but also for all of us. Throughout his ministry, the central message of Jesus was the "good news" that God's reign was already dawning.

Paradise is the advent of God's presence in our lives. But can we experience what Jesus promised when our world and our lives are so opposed to its fulfillment? As we move toward the second millennium after Jesus' death, what can we expect? How can we live out this expectation in faith and trust?

Blind faith in some future life is not the answer. The world is too burdensome; it grinds us down too incessantly for such a "pie-in-the-sky" spirituality. Such a path can only lead us toward an impotent, zestless life. This is not our calling.

We need a more vibrant hope, a hearty faith built upon a

spirituality firmly rooted in our lives and the world around us, and born of a true conversion. We pray: "Turn us, O Lord, back to you. Break us open once again, and fill us with your grace so that we might truly live."

We cannot force this conversion; all we can do is slow down enough to be able to hear God inviting us to turn around. This grace will come, gentle and insistent, quietly beckoning us to embrace it. We turn toward God, not on our own initiative, but in response to God's.

But one-time conversion is not enough, for we sin again and again, failing to live out the love to which God calls us. So, though our spirituality will be born of conversion, it will be nurtured by a life of prayer.

Our prayer must not consist simply of forced, arid supplications that we frequently offer because we should. Instead, it is to be a response to the God who has spoken to us first. Prayer needs to be the light that guides us; it needs to be the very life we live, because it is the truest part of our being.

This vibrant spirituality infects our whole way of being. It is not the too-happy, too-shallow life of those who escape from life's burdens. Rather, it undergirds a life of integrity and freedom that accepts the heavy burdens of life and carries them gracefully, buoyantly.

As the light of prayer illumines more and more of our lives, we see the face of God in the joy, suffering, and struggle of people everywhere. We are made vigorous by these flesh-and-blood encounters with God among us. Joyously, we help others shoulder their burdens just as they help us shoulder ours.

These are the fruits of the paradise the dying Jesus promises, not only a paradise in some mystical world beyond death, but a beautiful garden in our lives here and now, where God's reign breaks open and blossoms. This is not an easy paradise without struggle, but a very real world of delight blossoming in the midst of thorns.

Holy One,
  I hold both good and evil within my disabled spirit.
  Without you, Jesus, the evil would devour the good.
But you outwitted and vanquished evil
  by your death.

Your cross reaches to heaven.
  Its arms extend to hold me close
  so the good within me might surface
    with power and love.

In the future,
  Messiah, Holy One,
    when evil beckons with its silky promises,
    turn me around,
    renew me,
    transform me,
    caress me with your grace.
I, too, wish to live in paradise with you.

8

*After that, Jesus, realizing that everything was now finished, said
to fulfill the Scriptures, "I am thirsty."* (John 19:28)

I am thirsty!

I came to be the living water,
to inundate the hardened heart.
    Instead, I hang powerless,
    for my fountain has dried up.
        I am thirsty!

Baptized, I rose from the Jordan
    to bring salvation through this cleansing,
        but today upon my gallows
        my broken body is drained.
            I am thirsty!

Sustained by flowing water and the Spirit,
    I prayed and taught and healed and loved.
    But now, emptied of all sustenance,
    I find the tide has turned away from me.
        I am thirsty!

The agony of estrangement
   burrows into my spirit.
The affliction of deprivation
   overwhelms my consciousness.
The burden of oppression
   torments my very being.
      I am thirsty!

———————————

Jesus cries out, "I am thirsty," expressing the agony of the one who suffers. This cry rises out of the depths of Jesus' being, "I suffer; I am in need." It is the primal scream of all suffering.

Jesus does not call for help, even less for an analysis of why there is suffering. Rather, he asks for recognition of his pain. If we yearn to follow him, we must hear his cry of thirst.

This cry echoes through the ages in the voices of all who thirst and hunger, or who ache for companionship, freedom, or justice. It is the scream of suffering in our world, echoing Jesus' agony on the cross.

If we are faithful, we must respond to this cry and alleviate misery. The strategy for this is a political and economic one, open to analysis and discussion. But the misery itself is not for analysis. It is to be heard, absorbed, and recognized as holy ground.

Many of us have forgotten how to recognize this holy ground. Once we have acknowledged an authentic cry of suffering, we prefer to forget because it is easier. Whether or not to respond to it is no longer open to debate. This primal scream cuts through all debate, all politics, and all theology. It exposes the flesh and bones on the cross. "I am thirsty."

Even as Jesus rejoices at new freedoms in South Africa, Germany, eastern Europe, and the Soviet Union, he still cries out from the parched deserts of the world. His voice rushes toward us on the dry winds of militarism in Central America. His lips crack and bleed as the victims of AIDS draw their last breaths. In the midst of repression in the world he yearns for freedom.

These suffering people are manifestations of the Lord, truly the presence of God in our world and our lives. Although in our loneliness and feelings of meaninglessness we thirst for consolation and ache for God's presence, we do not really want this suffering God. We would prefer an easier, more comfortable God.

But the God of the Israelite people, the God of Jesus, is not a convenient or "cozy" God, but Emmanuel: God-with-us-always. This God is present when the goodness of life spills over and satiates us, but also when we have periods of unquenchable thirst. This God promises to be with us especially in our fears and in the suffering of the lowly and afflicted.

Why do we feel that our lives have to be in perfect control before we will trust God and serve others? Why do we, citizens of the wealthiest society in history, feel unable or unwilling to face the sufferings and needs of others? Although we live well in our overextended and harried lives, we feel immobilized by the pain of others. As we race from one commitment to the next, our hectic "leisure" too often crowds out any chance to serve others.

This is a sign of how much we need conversion. If Jesus calls us clearly to one thing, it is to be available to serve others. That we feel so powerless, so overwhelmed by the world, says something about our world and ourselves.

We live in a world filled with monumental suffering, beyond any individual's ability to alleviate. But even as we recognize our limits, we need to strive to do what we can. If we thirst for a world in which service is encouraged and fruitful, we must help to build such a world.

Our powerlessness shows us something about ourselves as well: we constantly hide our withered hearts from those with whom we work, from our loved ones, even from ourselves. The sheer effort required to hide our forsakenness is draining us, sucking us ever more dry. The first step beyond this dryness is to admit our thirst, as Jesus does on the cross.

May we break open our lives before God, acknowledge the depth of our thirst, and serve others in theirs. In this conversion from isolation to shared thirst we will find the life-giving rain of the resurrection falling upon us, slaking our parched spirits. May we break open our dry ground and soak in the water of life.

Jesus,
> as I look upon your tortured form
> and see a broken cistern empty of all water,
> I wonder what hope there is for me,
>> a beggar for the trash of life,
>> tormented by the drought within?

I satiate myself
> with fraudulent ambitions.
I drink,
> I gulp polluted waters.
>> I am thirsty!

So frequently I am like Pilate,
    cleansing myself of guilt;
Like Peter,
    fearful, when I step into the water.

Perversely, I resist your washing of my feet.
Parched, I wander through the desert,
    passing by all wells of living water,
bearing the burden of my empty water jars.
    I am thirsty!

Yet, there you are,
    pinned down upon a precipice.
Your cross becomes a cataract,
    replenishing my spring
        and so
I have no reason to thirst,
    for your heart is pierced
    and I am refreshed once more.
        Your living water flows free again!

9

From noon onward, there was darkness over the whole land until midafternoon. Then toward midafternoon, Jesus cried out in a loud tone, "Eli, Eli, lama sabachthani?", that is, "My God, my God, why have you forsaken me?" (Matthew 27:45–46)

My God, my God, why have you forsaken me?

Is this what it means to be human:
    to be fettered like a villain to a tree?
    to ache with every twitch and spasm
    when my body is battered with my wounds?

Is this what it means to be human:
    to be tormented by isolation?
    to burn with doubts and insecurities
    when my heart is broken by my yearning?

Is this what it means to be human:
    to be immersed in extreme desolation?
    to long for deliverance and liberation
    when my spirit feels abandoned by all love?

Why do I feel excluded from all favor?

banished to a bottomless pit of torment?
convulsed by the terror of my emptiness?
Is this the price I pay for sin?

Abba, eternal lover, why does it seem
you have forsaken me?

Forsaken... abandoned... deserted... discarded.... How often do we feel the emptiness of these words ourselves? They instill a fear of being alone and lonely, reminding us of emptiness and meaninglessness.

Yet, these are also the words great mystical writers have used to express their journeys to God. Along with the mystics, the anonymous writers of black spirituals, Thomas Merton, Gustavo Gutiérrez, Dorothy Day, Martin Luther King, Jr., and others also attest to this painful encounter with God. Somehow, they came to hear God's voice in the kind of abandonment Jesus experienced on the cross. How are we to make sense of this paradox? How can the loneliness we fear so greatly become the place we hear God's voice?

Of course, we are not to seek abandonment and forsakenness, but life in all its fullness instead, in the multiplicity of its many colors. This fullness includes celebrating the goodness and grace that we discover in our efforts to love and to live well. But it also includes accepting, just as deeply, the times of trial and loneliness that seep into our lives. We would prefer not to enter into such trials when we are forced to drink from this cup.

This experience of isolation may come with the death of a loved one, the loss of a job, the severing of a relationship, the departure of children from home, or simply with the emptiness of the routine details of our daily existence.

We try to find ways to hide from such painful experiences. It makes little difference whether we deaden ourselves through alcohol or loveless sex, too much work or persistent laziness, or with any of the other myriad deceptions we find. The dynamic is the same: concealing our emptiness even from ourselves, we pretend it is not there. We cover it up or try to fill it with what is fleeting or insubstantial.

But the void remains. If neglected, the vacuum expands, sucking the very center of our existence into itself. This leads us to feel forsaken by our friends and loved ones. Godforsaken. Strangely, this most bitter of moments is also potentially the holiest. But to find the holy center of ourselves, we must enter into the vast desolation we fear within us. Only there will our illusions be burned away and their ashes carried off by the tears that flow from within and without.

One of the first illusions to fall away is that of self-sufficiency. The reality is, we are not self-sufficient; we need God and we need others to help us see God. We feel abandoned not because God leaves us, but because we leave God. The choices we make—as individuals, communities, and as a nation—leave us isolated and fearful, unable to see God's will.

Jesus feels forsaken on the cross, not because he leaves God but because he is discarded and put to death by a world threatened by his message. And Jesus is abandoned daily when we fail to love one another, when we do not extend a hand of consolation to those around us.

Our vocation is nothing short of this: to transform the world of death around us, especially in working with those who suffer far more than we: the poor, the outcast, the sick, the hungry, the homeless in our neighborhood and around the world.

When we cry out, "My God, my God, why have you for-saken us?" God will surely answer us, console us, if we will allow it. But part of God's consolation may surprise us as we are called to respond to the nagging question: "My child, my child, why have you forsaken me?"

Jesus, Savior,
  humanity's a heavy burden.
To taste its ugliness and sin
  gnaws at our hearts and nerves and spirits,
  inviting resistance from within.

Yet, we find hope through your identification
  with our weak human nature.
  You've known our depths of degradation;
  You've become a martyr for our cause.

Abandonment's an ugly feeling,
  lodging torment in our depths.
  Since you've survived it with such valor,
  we turn to you in our need.

When we appeal for solace
  during our raw and painful moments,
  enfold us in your compassionate embrace,
    divine and loving friend.

Then, with your tender love as our support,
  alert us, sensitize us to the forsaken,
  the oppressed and the tormented
    in our midst.

May our presence and response
   witness to your sojourn among us.
Grant us release from the terror
   of abandonment.

10

When Jesus took the wine, he said, "Now it is finished." Then he bowed his head and delivered over his spirit. (John 19:30)

It is finished!

In time,
> Abba sent me forth
> > to become a human being
to bring the Holy One's message
> of love and salvation
> > to all on earth.

Throughout my very ordinary life
> while living in your midst,
I rejoiced in friendship, acceptance, love, and service.
I obeyed Abba
> and did the best I could to deliver the Good News.
I also let down my defenses
> to be one with you.
Inevitably, I suffered
> misunderstanding, rejection,

betrayal and abandonment.
I lived with integrity, mirroring the Holy One,
and so became a threat to those in power.

As I leave this earth,
much of humanity remains blind;
hatred fractures hearts;
pride ruptures the spirit.

But I can't be seduced
by apparent failure.
My life is finished.
I've done all that I was able to do.
As darkness enfolds me
and life seeps out drop by painful drop,
I grow weary.
Abba understands that I can no longer go on.
It is all over.
It is finished.

I end my time with you.
Eternity is calling;
I can't ignore its chorus.
I go content to meet the Holy One
who sent me forth
to establish the kingdom in your midst.
I am finished,
for the mustard seed has been planted,
the treasure hidden in a field.

So, as I bid farewell, I ask you
to take on my yoke,

to walk where I have walked.
I pass on to you the Holy One's desire
that love dominate the earth.

Accept this invitation
to complete the task that I've begun.
Believe in me;
have hope;
go forward.
I will be with you until the end of time.

"It is finished." Once, these final words of Jesus were considered a confident expression of a task completed, something like, "OK, Abba, I have fulfilled your will." It was as if Jesus felt that God wanted him to be crucified. But we should no longer understand these words this way. God is not a masochistic God who wants his son, or anyone else, to suffer. These are the dying words of a man too spent to continue, a human rag wrung out and left hanging in the breeze. They are not the words of a man suffering in order to fulfill God's will.

They reveal a far more real and challenging Jesus, for he is a Jesus much like us. God's will for him (and for us) was not that he suffer, but that he live with faith, hope, and integrity. Because he lived that way, he was crucified by a world that could not face the power of that integrity. And so, at the end, Jesus says in agony, "I can no longer go on, Abba; I am finished."

This understanding is vital if we are to follow Jesus authentically. For when we despair, we do not usually feel secure in having done God's will. We feel only the darkness and the narrow confines of our world and our sinfulness closing in upon us. That is why we lose hope.

At such moments, the dashed hopes of Jesus on the cross can come alive. He did not simply dance through life, always the confident one, any more than we do. On the cross, he shares our agony, our darkest moments. He offers our fears, along with his own, to God and gives us the faith to go forward. We need only accept this gift.

In such times of insecurity, God does not ask us to pretend that all is well, that we "have it all together." Instead, God beckons us to feel the oppressive blackness and even to have faith in grace. Jesus invites us to continue even when all seems truly lost, trusting him to break open the most tightly-closed spaces of our lives.

"I am finished. I cannot go on." Yet God carries us forward. This is our faith in the darkest of times, the bleakest of days. And as God carries us forward, we are nurtured until we can walk in the light once again.

There is much in life that overwhelms us, Lord.
    Wrong choices, misunderstandings,
    unsuccessful efforts, persistent demands
        crowd in
    and we struggle to discern
    what your will is for us.

We yearn for your guidance,
    yet we pursue our own desires.

We seek your friendship,
    yet we fear its intimacy.

We analyze your words,
    yet we ignore their summons.

We long for your love,
    yet we doubt it when offered.

We wince at your invitation to holiness,
    yet we need your blessings.

We flutter around in our search,
    wasting our time in non-essentials.

Why is obedience so difficult?
If we submit ourselves to you,
    do we give away our freedom?

The answer surfaces
    at the foot of your cross.

As you stretch there on your death bed
    whispering, "It is finished,"
    we sense your weariness.

Throughout your life you sought Abba's will,
    tirelessly moving forward,
    until your body, heart, and spirit
    were thoroughly spent.

Now your life is at an end
    and your wounded body craves release.

In freedom, you obeyed the one who sent you

with integrity and honor.
You became a threat to the status quo
and so you received the death sentence.
Your work is finished;
there is not much more that you can do.
So you must move on.

Lord, we, too, have experienced similar apprehension
and so we plead:
grant us courage, stamina, and determination
to work as tirelessly as you,
to accept wholeheartedly
the commandments of blessing and of love
you offered us
on the mounts of Galilee and Jerusalem.

As we respond to your invitation,
we beseech your help;
when forces buffet us, strengthen us
to carry out God's will
by freely choosing it.

Give us hearts
willing to be, to love, to serve
in moments of weakness and of strength,
at times of emptiness and of fullness,
during periods of discouragement and of blessing.

You took on the yoke of our humanity
and died battered and broken,
closing your life of pain.

We, too, accept the inevitable,
    believing that your love
    supports and comforts us
        when we follow you.

At our moment of death
    may we, too,
wearily and confidently say,
    "It is finished."

11

*It was now around midday and darkness came over the whole
land until midafternoon with an eclipse of the sun. The curtain in
the sanctuary was torn in two. Jesus uttered a loud cry and said,*
    "Father, into your hands I commend my spirit."
After he said this, he expired. (Luke 23:44–46)

———————

Into your hands I commend my spirit.

I choose the moment of my death.
    No one can take my life away from me
        unless I give it up.

I raise my head in final blessing.
As past and future merge into the present,
    my last moments freeze in time
        and chloroform the pain,
as sinew, bone, and blood
    articulate surrender.

———————

Here on the cross, Jesus hands over his spirit and his very
identity to the Holy One. In giving himself over in this ulti-

mate act of faith, he is our model for the offering up of our lives in faith, hope, and love.

This language of giving ourselves over to God is all around us recently. A popular religious poster exhorts us to "let go and let God." The 12-step programs for growing beyond our compulsions of alcohol, food, and sex ask us to accept our dependence on a Higher Power. In both public worship and private prayer, we follow Jesus in surrendering to God: "Your will be done."

This call beyond our false independence into true dependence on God cuts directly to the heart of our calling as human beings and as Christians. In their invitation to spiritual growth by acknowledging personal weakness, Alcoholics Anonymous and other support groups follow in the footsteps of the mystics throughout the ages. We need God—it is as simple as that.

But this truth that cuts so cleanly is a two-edged sword. Too often, in our yearning to rely on God, we refuse to take responsibility for our choices. One edge this truth reveals is the *childlike* heart of trust and hope in God as we make choices. The other edge is the *childish* heart that fantasizes that God makes choices for us.

The difference is this: the God of Jesus, the God proclaimed for centuries, is a God of freedom. We are free to choose—even to choose badly at times, falling into sin and fencing in our freedom. The god we make responsible for our choices is a different god, a false god created by our minds as we project our unhealthy dependence.

How can we tell the difference? The true God calls us to freedom and an ongoing relationship with the Holy One. The mark of this encounter is a growing sense of joy in accepting responsibility for one's life, even as this life is lived in search of God's will. It is marked, too, by the humility of recognizing that all is a gift of God.

The false god actually leads us into deeper dependence. Although this feels good at first, this god can never give us true freedom, for in worshipping such a god we worship ourselves. Also, such an encounter is marked by a growing fear and reluctance to accept responsibility for our actions. We would prefer to blame "god" for our failures, for the failures of others, for the way the world is.

Jesus makes his final commitment: "Into your hands I commend my spirit." In this commitment, Jesus invites us to hand over our spirits in total trust; this is a conversion once again to the true God of life. If we have given our hearts over to a false god, all is not lost. We are called once more to turn around, to give ourselves to the one true God who calls us to freedom and responsibility.

Such a conversion does not make life easy. As Jesus' death shows, giving ourselves to God does not mean our journey will be without suffering or pain. There will be times when we will not experience his presence supporting our freedom. But if we continue, always open to fuller conversion, the God of freedom will lead us onward, revealing the love and wisdom within our hearts. We will discover that this is the only path that leads to others and away from self-absorption.

You have redeemed me,
    faithful God, Holy One.

Exultantly, I proclaim your goodness!
    As I live out my life and await my death,
    I dedicate each of my moments

to your guidance and your will,
    committing my spirit,
    handing it over to you,
    the God of integrity and wholeness.

And whenever I am lifted up
    to hang upon my cross,
    may your courage seep into my heart.
Be present then with me.

I'm yours!
Now and forever.
    Into your hands I commend my spirit!

12

On the first day of the week, at dawn, the women came to the tomb bringing the spices they had prepared. They found the stone rolled back from the tomb; but when they entered the tomb, they did not find the body of the Lord Jesus. While they were still at a loss over what to think of this, two men in dazzling garments stood beside them. Terrified, the women bowed to the ground. The men said to them: "Why do you search for the Living One among the dead? He is not here; he has been raised up." (Luke 24:1–6)

My temple that evil destroyed so cruelly
    was rebuilt within the promised timetable.
I rose, glorified and transfigured,
    leaving you behind
    to carry to the ends of the earth
    the good news of my love, acceptance, and forgiveness.

Yet, I remain with you always,
    to roll away whatever stones entomb your spirit
    so you might enjoy a new life with me.

I'll hide in a variety of disguises to eliminate your fears, hoping your trust will transform them into wonder.

I'll walk with you along your road
  to sanctify it, make it holy ground.

I'll break your bread and drink your wine
  to fill you with my power.

I'll slip through the locked door of your heart
  to replenish it with courage.

Don't falter.
  Dig your fingers into my wounds.
  Believe in me.
I've triumphed over death to prove my love.

I command you:
  Break through your tomb;
  be a witness to the miracle of grace I leave you.

Remember, you are incomplete
  until you accomplish the task
  that is your destiny.

Provide me with the opportunity I need
  to continue teaching and healing
  this disjointed world.

Soar to a higher level,
  be glorified with me!

There once was a man who lived so fully that he was either loved or despised by all those who knew him. A fire of love burned brightly at the core of his being, and so people came to warm themselves near him. His very presence was a respite from a cold world that otherwise offered no home. He was the chastening fire of life, the warm milk of love.

But one day he was assassinated by those who could not stand the light of his fire. His followers, feeling abandoned and alone, despaired of all hope. They wandered, fragmented and lost, in a world without meaning.

Some were lost that way forever. But soon those who continued to search for meaning began to feel the stirrings of new life within them. At first, very subtly, new hope was born. Then quickly, urgently, as they came together and shared the man's story, he became once again the overwhelming center of their lives—as individuals and as a community. That quickening within, that strange movement of new life, was not just recovery from the grief of having lost their beloved Jesus. It was more, much more. Something burned within them, firing their hearts.

"Could it be? It's impossible! He's dead and buried. But, yes, it is the Lord living among us, setting our hearts aflame once again, burning even more intensely than before. It is beyond words, indescribable...but somehow, somehow, he is back here among us, fully present and fiercely alive. Alive!"

Although his presence gradually faded, somehow he left with them the gentle breath of his Spirit. From time to time, that Breath would rise up and rekindle the flame of his love within them, letting them know that indeed he had risen and was still in their midst.

The gospels tell us precious little about Jesus' resurrection. Only in the evocative language of mystery could the first Christians speak of their experiences of Jesus, the crucified-yet-still-among-us. It is this mystery that we are left to ponder and to celebrate at Easter.

But we need to do more than ponder; we need to open ourselves to that same breath of the Spirit and allow it to rekindle among us the flame of Christ's love.

Lord, as the women were going to your funeral,
    they were worried about your last anointing.
They did not realize that it had already been done
    the week before by the prostitute
    who had "wasted" aromatic myrrh on you.

But having broken the bonds of death,
    you were wandering, searching
    for a haven within the heart of humanity.

Today, you continue pursuing us with your surprises,
    for nothing can impede you.
You ignore walls and closed doors
    to stand in the midst of frightened friends.
You invite the doubting to finger your wounds
    so they might have security of heart and mind.

You come and go,
    choosing the people, places, and times
    to make yourself visible and known.
Your friends respond with love.

As you roam our world today,

glorious but obscure,
you become
>   visible to those with eyes to see,
>   available to those with ears to hear,
>   present to those with hearts to love.

You are one with the homeless,
>   living under their bridges and in their cardboard boxes.

You stroll along our Emmaus roads
>   when we are depressed and faithless.

You prepare breakfast in our kitchens
>   and sit at the helms of our boats.

You are alive and in our midst,
>   but we ignore you
>   as if you are still buried in your cave.

Resurrected Christ,
>   pierce our darkness with your light
>   and lift us out of our abyss of apathy.

Help us accept your companionship;
>   comfort us, embrace us
>   as we huddle in our loneliness.

May we acknowledge you as the Lord of our lives!

13

The eleven disciples made their way to Galilee, to the mountain to which Jesus had summoned them. At the sight of him, those who had entertained doubts fell down in homage. Jesus came forward and addressed them in these words:

> *"Full authority has been given to me*
> *both in heaven and on earth;*
> *go, therefore, and make disciples of all the nations.*
> *Baptize them in the name*
>   *of the Father,*
>   *and of the Son,*
>   *and of the Holy Spirit.*
> *Teach them to carry out everything*
>   *I have commanded you.*
> *And know that I am with you always,*
>   *until the end of the world!" (Matthew 28:16–20)*

My beloved ones,
   the time has come to say goodbye.
It is a painful moment
   both for you and me.
I have been with you sharing myself,

inviting you to friendship,
loving you,
challenging you,
teaching you about Abba.

What have you learned from me?
    What kind of friends are you?
Will you go to the far corners of your earth
    to share the love that Abba has for you?

If I were not to leave you,
    you would continue to depend upon me as a teacher.
So I lay the task
    of teaching and witnessing on you,
    trusting that, in the Spirit,
    you will capture my spirit
        to set it free to enflame the earth
        with light, and love, and power.

Farewell.
    Walk my way and I will be with you
        even when you can no longer see me
        nor feel my presence.

Eventually, when your task is done,
    we will greet each other
    in joy and recognition.

I wait with hope 'til then.

The early Christian communities proclaimed their utter
confidence in the salvation brought by the One in whose

name they gathered, Jesus the Christ. They felt Jesus' presence in their daily lives as he proclaimed his power: "full authority...make disciples of all the nations...baptize them... and know that I am with you always, until the end of the world."

We gather in the name of this same Jesus Christ. Do we also feel this power flowing into us with the breath of the Spirit? Are we empowered when we encounter Jesus in the Word as written in Scripture and made flesh in our lives? Are we energized when we welcome Jesus in the eucharist, when we strive to love?

But seeking this encounter with Jesus is risky, for it is always precarious to trust another. Called repeatedly to accept God's unlimited love, revealed to us in Jesus and given freely by the Spirit, we yearn for God's presence. But we have been so battered in our attempts to love and be loved, to give ourselves to others and to accept them unconditionally, that as a result we are afraid to trust and we close ourselves off from God's love. Although we thirst, we also run from the promise of living water.

Yet God breaks in. The first Christians experienced this and staked their lives on it. They trusted. As a result, God entrusted them with a mission "to all nations" and empowered them to carry it out.

"Full authority"—Do we exercise it? Not the authority that dominates others nor the arrogance that relies solely on self, but the authority that carries a confidence built on trust in God. It invites others to experience this same confidence.

"Baptize them"—Do we allow God to baptize us continually in the waters of trust, the waters that erode our fears as they flow gently in our lives? Do we call others to this same baptism?

"Make disciples"—Do we live out the faith we have been given in ways that declare God's love and the hope that is in us? Do our lives draw others to encounter this same spirit of love?

If we have the faith to do these things, we have a promise: "I am with you always, until the end of the world." In the freedom of this promise, our lives are made new.

Like gravity, Jesus,
    my helplessness and impotence
    draw me to you.
I insist you remain.
    I do not want to let you go.
    It is so comfortable having you around.

Goodbyes are difficult.
    They stab my heart like wounds.
Yet, you ignore my pain and,
    calling me by name,
    commission me to take your place.

As you bid me leave
    the personal enclave of my resistance,
    I struggle, hesitate.

How worthy am I to be
    your light or love or power?

Thundering from the mountain top,
    reverberating through my divided heart,
    your invitation urges:
    "Be in the world for me."